Gettysburg's
Haunted Address

SPIRITS OF
FARNSWORTH HOUSE INN

Compiled and Edited by
Bernadette Loeffel-Atkins

ISBN-978-1-57747-140-0

Cover photos by Helen S. Schwartz

Cover design by René Staub

Dedication

To the memory of
Michael F. Mattingly
Sherry Marie Miller

Contents

Acknowledgements

I would like to thank Loring and Jean Shultz, caretakers of the Farnsworth House Inn for the past thirty years and their daughter Patti S. O'Day, known as the "Ghost Mistress of Gettysburg" for offering me the opportunity to compile the stories of their haunted inn. Special thanks go to Master Storyteller René Staub for his wonderful ideas and tales from the inn as well as his artistic flair with the cover design. To photographer Helen S. Schwartz and her assistant Gail Kehler, thank you for your patience and for all the wonderful photographs. And to my daughter Beth Atkins, thanks for assisting me in this endeavor. To all of those who have shared their stories and experiences with the Farnsworth House Inn, we thank you. And last but not least, I thank our highly spirited residents for making the Historic Farnsworth House Inn such an interesting place to visit and to work.

Jim Thomas photo

Introduction

Adams County, Pennsylvania has always been rich in history and folklore. From the stories of the Native Americans, the German and Scotch-Irish Settlers, to the bloody three day battle, history and tales of excitement and terror were spun together to create entertaining, suspenseful stories. Recollections and reminiscences of olden times have been passed on through generations to be retold. Today, at 401 Baltimore Street, the Historic Farnsworth House Inn continues the tradition of storytelling at their Civil War Mourning Theatre and Haunted History Candlelight Ghost Walks.

In 1972, Loring and Jean Shultz purchased what is now known as the Farnsworth House Inn from Sara Black Gideon. The Shultz's daughter, Patti O'Day was 14 years old at the time of the purchase. During the early years, Patti could sense the feeling of spirits around her, but did not witness anything unusual. As the years passed, the visuals and spirituous sensations became more frequent.

Jim Thomas photo

In the early days of storytelling in the cellar of the Farnsworth House, Patti would have people from the audience speak to her following the show. Many were former boarders of Sara Black Gideon. Patti started collecting the stories and became intrigued with the history of the house.

In 1986, Ms. O'Day started telling ghost stories in the cellar of the Farnsworth House Inn. Dressed in her Civil War period "Widow's Weeds" and black mourning veil, Patti descended into the darkness of the 19th Century viewing parlor and captivated her audiences with tales of the unknown and phantom specters that still haunt the inn, town and battlefield. The Farnsworth House Inn is where modern day ghost story telling began in Gettysburg. Patti O'Day is affectionately referred to as the "Ghost Mistress of Gettysburg."

At the present time, there are 14 resident restless spirits roaming the house and grounds of the Farnsworth House Inn. Many have names and distinctive personalities, others are nameless and prefer to just watch the mortal world go by around them. At one time, there were 16 spirits living in the house. A few years ago a "ghost release" ceremony was performed and the ghosts were offered the chance to pass through the veil. Only two took them up on their offer.

Farnsworth House Inn is listed as one of the most Haunted Inns in America. The Inn has been featured on the Travel Channel, A & E, as well as the Sci-Fi Network and a host of others.

Helen S. Schwartz photo

"Ghost Mistress" Patti O'Day in the Mourning Theater.

The "Residents"

The creaking sound of footsteps in the hallway, the impression of someone sitting on a bed, a feather-like touch on one's face, a crying child, a laughing child, a whispering voice, this is the Farnsworth House Inn. The inn's ghostly inhabitants include Civil War soldiers, a midwife, at least three children and a few mystery ladies.

Mary — A matronly woman that keeps the other ghosts in line and visits with any visitors that are under the weather.

Walter — A curmudgeonly red-bearded Confederate Civil War soldier.

Nan — A nurse midwife.

Billy — A little boy from the 1950s who grew up to be a man but never had a childhood.

Jeremy — The little boy who was tragically killed by a horse-drawn carriage in the 1800s.

Cissy — A little girl from the early 1900s with long curly blonde locks. She died from respiratory failure.

Florence — A 19-year-old woman who gave birth to a stillborn baby.

Elizabeth (Lizzie) — The ghost who moved into the house with her mortal family. She died in 1883.

Lt. Jackson — Cared for mortally wounded comrade in the cellar.

Dying Comrade — His painful cries are heard in the cellar.

William — Jeremy's grief-stricken father.

Jennie Wade — Twenty-year-old Gettysburg civilian believed to be killed by a sharpshooter from The Farnsworth House Garret.

❖ *The remainder of our spirits are known only to God* ❖

There was something awesome in the thought of the solitary
mortal standing by the open window
and summoning in from the gloom outside
The spirits of the nether world.

Sir Arthur Conan Doyle

The Sara Black Room

Sara Black Gideon, former owner of what is now known as the Farnsworth House Inn has one of the Bed and Breakfast rooms named in her honor. This highly spirited room has become a popular haunt for ghost hunters and tourists alike. At one time, this room was the master bedroom of the house and the bathroom was the nursery. It is in the hall near these two rooms that a number of guests witnessed a rather tall gentleman dressed in turn-of-the-century (1890s) clothing wearing a high collar and cravat. The grief-stricken man is heard to be mournfully sobbing.

Farnsworth House Ghost Mistress, Patti O'Day recalls that a psychic friend of hers believed that the sorrowful man seen in the house is the father of the spirit of a little boy who frequents the Farnsworth House. The story is told that a little boy was struck by a horse drawn carriage and crushed in front of the house on Baltimore Street while playing "horse tag" with his friends. His father ran from the house, picked up the limp and battered body of his son and carefully carried him to the nursery. It is believed that the father refused to release his son's lifeless body and the child had to be forcibly taken from him.

This child spirit is approximately 4 to 6 years old and is affectionately known as Jeremy. Jeremy is a playful spirit, he sings Christmas carols, giggles and chases his ball around the hallway of the house.

Jeremy has become a popular fixture at the Farnsworth House Inn. Well-wishers bring him toys and candy. In return, Jeremy entertains them with his antics, hiding cell phones, stacking coins on the dresser, unplugging the alarm clock, turning water faucets on and his voice has been recorded numerous times.

The Sara Black room itself is highly active with spirits. On numerous occasions, the wedding dress in the corner of the room has become highly animated with the sleeves of the dress flailing around wildly through the air. Spirits have been photographed near the bed and people from outside claim to have seen a little boy hanging out of the window of the Black room, gleefully watching a parade go by on Baltimore Street.

Stories From The Sara Black Room

- "Around 3:00 in the morning my husband woke up with a tickling cough. As he was getting settled back into a peaceful sleep, a woman distinctly whispered a few words in his ear. It was a voice he never heard before..."

- "Our lamp turned itself on and off. When we went over to investigate, it was unplugged.... As a joke I said, *Hello Jeremy.* Imagine my surprise when a child's laugh responded!"

- "Last night, as we were trying to sleep, we started to hear strange knocking. It was around 4 a.m...for nearly an hour we listened to the knocking...tap tap tap tap...we were the only ones in the house...or were we?"

- "Around 3:30 in the morning, I woke from a dead sleep, smelling roses. Later I woke up in a cold sweat with someone tapping me on the back five times. Then I heard voices...."

- "We re-entered our room and heard a child laughing, but saw nobody. Around 2:50 a.m., tapping around corner of room awakened me. I heard a ball bounce, knocking on the window and later, pacing outside our door. We heard voices in the corner where the wedding dress is located. We felt something hard bump on the bed. Whatever it was, it was sitting on the edge of our bed."

- "Last night was terrifying. I suddenly awoke to the floor creaking right next to my bed. I kept my eyes shut...the whole bed jumped as if someone picked up the headboard and let it go!"

- "We set up a digital voice recorder on the table at the foot of the bed. I placed some toys with the recorder. The next morning after listening to hours of nothing, I heard a voice say *Jeremy*. A few minutes later, the voice again, *Red Box...*" *(The Red Box sometimes has little toys in it for Jeremy.)*

- "Around 4 a.m. we heard clicking noises in the room. It sounded like the noise that children's wooden blocks make when banged together. Was Jeremy playing with his blocks?"

- "Right outside of our room, the boar's head was wildly swinging back and forth on the wall. The group stood and watched in disbelief. I had to grab it to make it stop moving."

Jeremy's blocks, like most little boys, he cannot spell his name.

The wild boar head located near the Sara Black room. It is said that wild boars fed on many of the dead soldiers.

Jim Thomas photo

- "A sound came from the dresser drawer like someone was trying to open it." *(Jeremy's toys are kept in that drawer.)*
- "The water faucet kept on turning itself on and off all night."
- "I awoke to the sound of footsteps pacing back and forth in front of the dresser. The knob was jiggling like someone was trying to open the drawer."
- "The foot of the bed lifted as if someone was trying to make the bed."
- "I spoke to Jennie Wade. She told me that she lived in town."
- "I awoke at 2:30 a.m. to the sound of tapping in front of the dresser. Was it Jeremy playing with his toys? Also woke up to the water faucet running in the bathroom."

Jim Thomas photo

The drawer where guests leave toys for Jeremy.

13

A Night In The Black Room

As told by Helen S. Schwartz

Sept. 3

I am spending the night in the Sara Black Gideon Room in the main house at the Farnsworth House Inn. It is me and four other friends staying in the rooms upstairs for the night. We are the only five people staying in this house tonight. I decided to write my impressions while the night goes on. It is around 2:00 a.m. I have been working on some photos on my computer for a couple hours, was seated on the bed beside the fireplace with the computer on my lap. While working I heard voices that seemed to come from the bathroom area...loud but muffled so that I couldn't make out the words...like if you hear a loud T.V. or conversation from another room next to yours through the wall but cannot make out the words. There were several voices...one louder than the rest...but all pretty loud...yelling, crying, clearly upset and disturbed situation. A lot of commotion. I thought that maybe my friends in the Sweney Room had the T.V. on too loud or something...only the sound was coming from my bathroom area and the Sweney Room is behind me. I continued to work, heard the voices stop and then start and then stop...then again

Farnswoth House Inn photo

Photo in the Sara Black room with mist appearing near the bed.

14

Helen S. Schwartz photo

The highly "spirited" wedding dress in the Sara Black room.

with arguing, crying, yelling...then it stopped. I looked at the clock...around 12:30am.... I had to recharge the battery in the computer so I went into the bathroom and plugged it in and then got back into bed. A bit later the voices started up again...loud again but still muffled so I couldn't make out definite words...was now 1:30am.... More fighting, crying, yelling.... I then heard a sound like a bang and then I felt a discomfort on either side of my head next to my eyes which then went away...and the voices stopped. I stayed awake for the remainder of the night...in the morning, I checked with my friends in the Sweney Room and they said they only had the T.V. on for a bit with the Food Network on and that there wasn't any loud yelling or crying or anything going on...nor were they creating any noise.

Morning, Sept. 4

We all were packing our stuff to move on to another room outside the main house for the next night and at one point there was only myself, and two friends in the house. We stood at the top of the stairs outside the Black and Sweney Rooms with our bags.... All three of us heard from the two rooms...click, click, click, click...the sounds of deadbolts being locked...we looked at one another and confirmed that we all heard the same things...and then one of us looked at the space under the Sweney Room door to see if there was anything visible and didn't see anything so we went down the steps and left.

The bathroom in the Sara Black room, formerly a nursery to the master bedroom.

Merry Christmas, Jeremy

As told by Bernadette Loeffel-Atkins

It was a cold December day and Winter had officially arrived just the day before. A gentleman and his son checked into the Sara Black room. It was an early Christmas gift to his son who had heard the stories of the Battle of Gettysburg and the tales of little Jeremy, the boy who tragically died in the room they were staying in. The excitement of the holidays was in the air and both father and son reveled in the thought of being on the battlefield together and sharing a real Civil War style dinner that evening.

After the night's festivities, the boy and his father settled in their cozy room for the evening. The little boy went through his nightly rituals of washing up and brushing his teeth. Unpacking his bag of toys and other goodies, the little fellow found a bag of Christmas candy that had been given to him by his Sunday School teacher. Dad gave him strict orders, "No candy until tomorrow!" The boy placed his bag of treats on top of the dresser where Jeremy's toys were secured in the drawer below.

The following morning, the groggy eyed little boy jumped out of bed and ran to the window to watch the twinkling of snowflakes fall and blanket the grassy patch in front of the inn. To his surprise, he had found his bag of candy opened and scattered all over the floor. The boy's father stirred in the bed and he sat upright. They heard a child's voice in the hallway singing, "I heard the bells on Christmas Day, the old familiar carols played, and wild and sweet the words repeat of peace on earth, good will to men."*

The little boy smiled, he knew that he had made a new friend.

* This song was written by Henry Wadsworth Longfellow in 1864 after learning that his son was missing in action during the Civil War.

The Catharine Sweney Room

Next to the Sara Black room is the Catharine Sweney Room, named after the former owner of the house during the Battle of Gettysburg. The spirits of Nan the midwife, Mary and Lizzie dwell in this area of the house. People who feel the presence of Nan the midwife experience a feeling of sadness. The midwife is heard pacing the floor all night.

The story is told that Nan was caring for a young woman named Florence who had just given birth to a still-born baby. One gets the sense that the midwife feels responsible for the death of the child.

On a dreary, cold Winter's day some years ago, a mother with her four year old daughter from Richmond, Virginia came to the Farnsworth House Inn. The daughter remained in the Sweney room playing with an antique mirror and brush on the floor while the ladies looked through the different rooms. The mother discovered that her daughter had vanished. Instant panic struck both the mother and Patti O'Day, who was taking them through the house. Moments later, Patti found the little girl crouched down behind a chair in the Sweney Room. When approached, the child cried out, "Oh, Mommy, the baby's dead!" Could this have been the stillborn baby who midwife Nan paced the floor over every night?

Vanity box containing the hand mirror and hair brush in the Sweney Room.

Helen S. Schwartz photo

19

- "We both woke up at 2:30 a.m. hearing continual pacing outside of our room."

- "...the footsteps continued all night (past 3:00 a.m.) We heard someone jiggle our lock from <u>inside</u> the room..."

- "In the middle of the night, I woke up smelling a strong, sweet, flowery scent for about a minute. My son smelled cigar smoke in the hallway."

- "My sister woke in the middle of the night and saw a face hovering over my waist. At first she thought it was me until she realized that my head was further up near the headboard. She turned back and the face was gone."

- "My wife heard some men's voices late into the night but decided to keep her eyes shut in fear of seeing something. She felt someone sitting at the foot of the bed."

- "I awoke to find the empty candy jar perched atop the vanity set. It was sitting on a wooden box when I went to sleep. Someone was playing a game, as the night before I kept putting it back in the right spot and the jar kept on being moved."

Helen S. Schwartz photo

The "moving" candy jar in the Sweney Room.

20

- "I was feeling very weary so I took a nap. Five minutes into the nap I felt someone patting the side of my head as to say, *There, there, you'll feel better.* "

- "I heard the lock on the door jiggle, I did smell roses and the bed shook a bit."

- "We heard what sounded like a hard ball being dropped down 2 or 3 stairs coming from the closet…it happened around 2:00 a.m. Goodbye Jeremy, have fun!"

- "There was a determined shaking and rattling of the door as if someone inside wanted out."

- "I was speaking to the spirits and a child's voice said, *Pop, is that you?* I later learned of Jeremy and his fate. Perhaps he was looking for his father."

- "We got the distinct scent of peppermint for about a minute and it disappeared. We later discovered that peppermint oil was used in handkerchiefs to cover up the stench of death."

- "We had an overall weird vibe in the room and several times it felt as if someone was sitting at the edge of the bed. During the night, the covers were pulled over my husband's head."

- "The door slammed by itself twice…I felt like I was being held down during the night. The faucet turned on by itself and the door rattled often. I heard footsteps in the attic around 4:00 a.m."

- "Around 3:15 a.m. I was awoke by a heavy pressure on the back of my head and neck. I tried to turn to awaken my friend, but was unable to move for a few moments. Later we heard running water in the bathroom. Footsteps were heard in the attic and a woman's voice was heard in the hallway…"

- "I left my jewelry in a small bag. In the morning I found it on top of the jewelry box."

- "Around 11 p.m. we heard footsteps…they continued all night. We heard someone jiggle our locks from inside the room. Then we heard a dull thud and a sliding sound coming from the attic. It sounded like someone sliding a heavy piece of furniture across the floor."

- "I woke up in the middle of the night to the smell of a sweet, strong, flowery scent. It only lasted a minute then disappeared."

- "About 2:30 a.m. we heard heavy foot steps in the attic as if a man was walking back and forth. It was very loud. Boom, boom, boom, boom and then back again."

- "I opened the fancy vanity box on the dresser which contained an antique brush, mirror and comb. As I picked up the mirror, an overwhelming stench of death filled the room. When I closed it, the stench went away."

- "As I lie in bed, a long streak of white light flashed over my head from the doorway and out the window. It was almost like a shooting star."

While yet a boy I sought for ghosts,
And sped through many a listening chamber. Cave and ruin,
And Starlight wood, with fearful steps pursuing
Hopes of high talk with the departed dead.

Percy Bysshe Shelley

The Cellar

On July 4th, 1863, Catharine Sweney and her daughter Elizabeth returned to their home to find broken windows, disarray and blood spattered everywhere. Elizabeth found a trail of blood that led her and her mother down to the cellar. In what is now called the catacombs, it is there that they discovered the body of a soldier resting atop the cool earth. Next to him was the shallow grave of his comrade, lying with a gaping wound to the neck, one that had nearly decapitated him.

Today, the cellar of the Farnsworth House Inn is still alive with the spirits of the past. The cheerful laughter and haunting image of Jeremy can be seen and heard in the cellar. A young boy can often be seen peering through the rafters, could this be Jeremy enjoying the evening entertainment?

It is told that Jeremy loves to play pranks on the guests. One evening a woman lunged out of her chair screeching at the top of her lungs — one by one, women jumped from their seats in a wave formation screaming. It seems that Jeremy was having a good time grabbing their ankles.

The following night, although not as vocal, Jeremy proceeded to grab ankles and tug on the pant legs of women in the audience. Another night Jeremy was pulling the hand of a woman in the audience. He was giggling and trying to persuade her to go to the front of the room. Jeremy also has a passion for untying shoelaces. Many people that experience the spirit of Jeremy work in caring professions. Jeremy is drawn to nurses, school teachers and guardians of some sort. Tugging on pant legs, being tickled by a pussy willow branch, these are all the doings of little Jeremy.

During a number of performances, the vision of a lady in a white dress has been seen peering at the audience from a quiet corner in the cellar. She is described as a middle-aged woman with brown hair that is pulled back. She wears a long flowing white dress with a high neck collar in a spider web design. All who have witnessed the spirit of this woman agree that her eyes were blue and could feel them piercing into their souls as she gazed upon them. This same spirit has been seen with her face pressed upon the glass of the bay window of the tavern.

One cool, crisp autumn evening as the sun set and the candles were lit in the cellar, a sensitive medium approached one of the storytellers and inquired, "Why is the name Abraham so near and dear to Mary's heart." Mary the matriarch ghost, has been seen in the cellar on numerous occasions. Mary, described as a small elderly woman with a dowager's hump can be seen roaming the halls and rooms of the Farnsworth House Inn. While in her presence, one is overwhelmed by the smell of roses. She has been called the Guardian Angel of the inn, the caregiver and she keeps the other spirits in line! In essence, Mary is the "House Mother." It is Mary's hand that caresses one's head or hand, and sits beside weary or ill visitors attempting to comfort them.

Stories are also told of a Lieutenant Jackson who brought his mortally wounded comrade to the cellar from across the street. As the soldier lay dying, the Confederate Lieutenant sang, "Just Before the Battle, Mother" to comfort his friend during his last moments of life. Today, visitors still hear the sorrowful tune being hummed throughout the house.

Stories From The Cellar

- "My earrings were tugged at and I was poked in the back. I can officially say that your cellar is haunted!"

- "My husband felt something sit down beside him, lean on his shoulder and he felt whiskers scratch the side of his face."

- "I felt something brush against my leg, and tap me on the shoulder. It gave me goose bumps!"

- "The two chairs next to us moved but nobody was sitting on them!"

Helen S. Schwartz photo

24

The Lieutenant

As told by Patti O'Day

Shaun did not know what to expect when he entered the cellar of the Farnsworth House for the first time to attend a show in the Mourning Theater. It was 11 p.m. and the Confederate gravesite tour was beginning. Shaun was dressed as a Confederate Lieutenant, his insignia proudly displayed on his gray uniform. The lights went out and the candles flickered eerily, making the shadows on the walls and ceiling seem larger than normal.

Then Shaun remembered a story about the staircase, the main one that lead to the upstairs landing and ultimately to the attic stairs. A child's carriage, constructed of metal and leather that sat on the landing outside the Sara Black room had moved mysteriously, it was facing in a different direction and two of its wheels were resting on the steps leading up to the garret. No one was around who could have moved the object without the team of investigators noticing. Later through psychic information, they found out that it was indeed little Cissy who wanted the carriage in the attic for her doll babies to travel in. As she started to climb the stairs, she ran out of energy and expressed sincere appreciation to who ever could make sure the carriage would finish its journey into the attic. The Lieutenant tried to clear his mind and be receptive to the tales the storyteller was weaving about the house.

The stories seemed to fly by without incident or disturbance and Shaun chuckled to himself, "Alright with the force." Just as the thought subsided, the audience began clapping for the storyteller. Doors opened and people started ascending the cellar steps. Shaun stayed behind to speak to the storyteller, Dave. "I would like to see the catacombs," the words just issued forth. "No, we normally do not allow people to walk into them" responded Dave. Shaun was disappointed and Dave noticed. Finally Dave agreed to allow him to step into the catacombs. Shaun was perfectly alright until the air seemed to have a mind of its own and started to press hard against his upper body. Suddenly, there seemed to be a hand pressed against his chest and he found it hard to breathe, very hard indeed.

He gasped, which caused Dave to turn toward him. The sleeves of his Confederate jacket seemed to move on his arms and right around his lieutenant insignia. They both noticed that the unseen fingers began to pick at the sewn on emblems as if it wanted them gone from the material altogether! Shaun shrieked and moved back a few steps. He opened his jacket to reveal a perfect red hand print across his chest! "Sweet Jesus, what the Hell was that all about?" cried the young man. Unknown to Shaun and Dave, a psychic who had originally investigated the attic found through Confederate sharpshooters who remained at their posts that there was a lieutenant in charge whom the men had no respect for.

The lieutenant had bumped his head on one of the rafters above while trying to obtain a vantage point for firing from the small window. The other soldiers had to stifle a laugh and both thought, "One of these days he'll get us all killed." Perhaps a shot in the back may be the solution to their problem. The psychic was totally bombarded with their total lack of respect for this lieutenant.

Dave gave a nervous laugh which seemed to hang in the air, "Maybe they just don't like lieutenants." Suddenly there was a tug at Shaun's pocket. Then he remembered, he was promoted to captain and his insignia was in his pocket! He fumbled and finally found the bars. Immediately he withdrew the insignia and pinned it to his uniform. Shaun covered the lieutenant insignia on his shoulders of his uniform. The abuse stopped immediately and a calm came over the room. It seemed both Shaun and the men in the garret were content with his promotion.

The Eternal Guardian

As told by Patti O'Day

It was on the eve before my 50th performance in the Mourning Theater. I had felt Mary's presence and the scent of roses on numerous occasions during presentations, but what was to happen that anniversary eve, nothing could have prepared me for what was to come for me or my guests that evening.

In telling the stories of the Battle of Gettysburg, I always began with Chamberlain's march to the town and Early's men who came from the west through Cashtown. Then I began to tell the story of the field itself and especially the Wheatfield, which I can no longer walk alone. The pain and suffering of individual soldiers trapped in the columns of wheat is truly unbearable, especially for an empathist like me. I started my story about how the wounded and dying laid on the field crying for water, for their mothers and for a God that they thought had forsaken them.

I was kneeling on the brick floor of the theater and as I rose slowly, my eyes looked back toward the undertaker sign on the back wall…there stood Mary. I had seen her before in the upstairs hallway not long ago. She appeared transparent, I could see the sign and stones of the wall through her body. Her gray hair pulled back at the nape of her neck, a dark dress and lighter colored apron. She was looking at me with soulful eyes and her expression was peaceful. I stood erect, forgot to breathe and quickly scanned the cellar to see if anyone was noticing, at least three or four couples were looking in the direction of my stance and definitely noticing! Then as quickly as she appeared, she disappeared.

I continued my storytelling with great difficulty, it seemed to never end, but during the time, I felt very at ease in my surroundings. The scent of roses became almost unbearable, and extremely pleasant at the same time. Immediately after the storytelling, a young man approached me. "Wow, great special effects," as he peered up at the rafters, "Where's the camera? Best 3-D effects I've seen in a long time." I paused, I did not want to divulge what I had seen. I responded, "What do you mean? What did you see?"

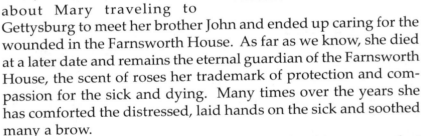

The young man responded, "A woman in a black dress, didn't you?"

Two other couples started talking with excitement, "We saw her too!" I asked them to describe her and if they heard anything. She apparently was just standing there and listening to my stories. After a moment, I started to tell them about Mary traveling to Gettysburg to meet her brother John and ended up caring for the wounded in the Farnsworth House. As far as we know, she died at a later date and remains the eternal guardian of the Farnsworth House, the scent of roses her trademark of protection and compassion for the sick and dying. Many times over the years she has comforted the distressed, laid hands on the sick and soothed many a brow.

The boy looked absolutely awestruck, "You mean that woman is dead?" I responded that she has been dead for quite a long time. All at once the group of folks who had seen Mary hurried towards the door. In a matter of moments, I was "alone" in the cellar.

The Garret Room

During the Battle of Gettysburg, the attic of the Farnsworth House sheltered Confederate sharpshooters. It is believed that one of these sharpshooters accidentally shot 20-year-old Gettysburg civilian Mary Virginia "Jennie" Wade while baking bread at her sister's home. The sound of Confederate soldiers are often heard from the attic dragging trunks across the floor. Folks staying in the Sara Black Room and the Sweney Room hear the sound of footsteps and music coming from the garret.

The sharpshooters in the attic are still here and very active. Some say that you can hear one of the soldiers playing a Jew's harp to pass the time away. The most infamous of the Confederate soldiers is a red-bearded man named Walter. Walter has an attraction to the ladies. During attic tours, he enjoys poking the ladies, running his fingers up and down their spine, generally spooking the gals out of their wits!

STORIES FROM THE GARRET

- "About 5 minutes into the presentation, I felt a very light feeling move across the back of my neck. About a minute later it happened on the middle of my back."

- We went into the attic. I was sitting on the bench. I felt dizzy and off balance the entire time. I kept feeling pin pricks at the waistband of my jeans on my back. It felt like I was being poked with a sharp toothpick.

*A house is never still in darkness to those who
listen intently; there is a whispering in
distant chambers, an unearthly hand presses
the snib of the window, the latch rises.
Ghosts were created when the first man
awoke in the night.*

J.M. Barrie

Blood Mommy, Blood

As told by Patti O'Day

Young Daniel and his mother came to Gettysburg to learn more about the Civil War. They were guests in the Garret Room, which at the time was one of the Bed and Breakfast rooms at the inn. The attic was small but cozy. As a matter of fact, it was so small that there was no bathroom in the room. The bathroom was on the second floor of the house and is still there today.

After a long hot day of touring the battlefield, climbing rocks in Devil's Den and attending a re-enactment, Daniel's mother was looking forward to getting Daniel bathed and into bed so she could have some quiet time. Daniel decided that he was grown up enough to go downstairs and get washed up without his mother's assistance. He resisted her pleas to go with him, she finally relented and let him go downstairs on his own. He had won the battle. Armed with towels, toothbrush and other toiletries for his evening ritual, she gave strict orders to him, "Down to the bathroom and back, no fooling around!"

As she was turning down the bed and gathering things for her bath, she heard screaming coming from downstairs. She flew down the flight of stairs to the second floor where she found her son huddled against the wall and curled up in a fetal position. As she carefully approached him, she could hear him muttering, "blood, blood…"

After further investigation, Daniel's mother found no signs of injury or blood on her son. Other guests of the inn heard the commotion and gathered around the little boy. With no hesitation, Daniel pointed to the partially open bathroom door, looked up to his mother and cried out, "Blood Mommy, blood everywhere." A male guest reached for the bathroom door, Daniel seeing this let out a fearful cry and buried his head in his hands so he could not look upon the gruesome sight again. Daniel was moved to another room so he would not have to see what had upset him. A guest threw the bathroom door open and found nothing but a pristine white tiled bathroom, no blood anywhere.

You may think that this young boy's imagination got the best of him after hearing stories of blood, gore and death. One must understand that the garret bathroom sits right where the brick and wood sections of the house meet. This is where Mrs. Sweney discovered the bloody carnage on July 4th, 1863. Blood was dripping down the walls as though an animal had just been slaughtered. You see, young Daniel had stepped into that bloody room on July 4th, 1993, 130 years to the day. The veils of time had parted and the boy stepped back in time to witness the horrors of war first hand.

The bathroom where a young guest witnessed a
bloody scene from the past.

The sharpshooter window in the garret with a soldier's image reflected in the left side of the window. The enlarged detail (right) shows facial features and coat buttons.

Cissy's Doll

As told by Patti O'Day

In the cellar there used to be glass cases containing a variety of Civil War artifacts from the Gettysburg battlefield. In one of those cases there was a white porcelain doll's face found on the grounds of the Farnsworth House. I was always drawn to the eyes which were azure blue and absolutely mesmerizing for anyone who dared look at them for more than a moment.

Many times during my presentations in the Mourning Theater, people would almost gasp when they laid eyes on the alabaster face with it's all-knowing eyes. It was my belief that my parents found the object near the staircase (storm cellar stairs) leading into the back of the theater (the catacombs). This belief continued until I met Mary Downing. She is a woman who worked with spirits all of her life, mostly at archaeology sites. She said that she always brought the past to the present and managed to bring light to many "lives" who lived in the past, but influenced our lives today. Individuals with families, lovers and hopes for the future, all reaching for a woman who's compassion and sincerity spilled into the lives of others around her. She most certainly has earned the right to tell their stories. Who better to tell little Cissy's story than Miss Mary! The little girl known now as Cissy today was not known until her connection with the doll's face became known in this life.

Mary Downing walked into my life a few years ago, eager to tell me the names of the spirits who have shaped the Farnsworth House. Jeremy, the lieutenant, the sergeant, the sharpshooters, Walter, Mary, Elizabeth, and the list continues. Spirits, all playing roles, influencing my family and folks who have come to stay with us over the years.

One evening after the dining room emptied out and the Bed and Breakfast guests settled in for the night, Mary and I decided to spend some time in the attic with "the boys," a few Confederate sharpshooters who remained at their post for eternity. I told Mary how lively they were, moving large wooden trunks across the floor in order to render a good shooting position from the garret window. It was a very good vantage point to fire on Union troops on Cemetery Hill. They were firing at close range (610 ft.) at Union troops in and around the McClellan house, now the Jennie Wade House. In a hail of bullets, we believe, as others do, that the fatal shot fired into the door of the house may have killed Miss Wade.

The first staircase leading to the garret at the uppermost level of the house seemed to completely envelope Mary. I turned to see her staring at the pine floorboards at the foot of the staircase. I was surprised she said nothing about the black leather carriage, the one that we found had mysteriously moved to the stairs the week before.

We sluggishly climbed the staircase to the attic. I slid down the wooden benches near the other window in the attic and sat quietly waiting for Mary to get a "fix" on energy which had followed us upstairs, it was like carrying a small child. I still said nothing. I remained quiet while her face went through a series of smiles, uncertainty and finally understanding.

"You found an alabaster doll's face with 'China' blue eyes under this very floorboard." Mary's comment took me aback, I just stared. "No," I said, "We did find one but it was near the staircase leading into the cellar." "No, ask your parents where they found the object." Mary was absolutely convinced I was wrong concerning the details of the doll head's finding. I let it go, in my mind I wondered, "Who's dolly was it?" The sweet voice on an angel spoke to me, "It was my dolly." A little startled, I looked up at Mary to my left. She smiled and closed her eyes. "Her name is Cecelia, Cissy, she's four years old and she died, she could not breathe." It was not from tuberculosis, that Mary was sure of.

Mike Lyon's sketch

Cissy had long blonde curls and a white dress with blue satin ribbons and bows. I felt a small hand grasp mine and a flood of "child's" energy entered my body. I smiled but at the same time wanted to cry. Who was this precious innocent child whose life was cut short? Mary was sure that this was not the last time we would hear from our darling, she would manifest and show herself in another way. She did not know her father, but her mother was waiting for her somewhere else. At the moment, a young girl named Elizabeth would care for her. Sweet dreams, my little angel.

Almost a year to the date of meeting my little one, four girls came to Gettysburg to stay at the Farnsworth House Inn. They had made reservations for the Jennie Wade and Sweney rooms in the old section of the house. The night passed without incident. The girls took many photos of the rooms after the other people had checked out. Having to get on the road and finding no time to view the photographs, they packed up and headed to their vehicles. A four and one half hour drive awaited them so they decided to view the photographs on their way home. They had paid good money for their new digital camera and the photographs were brilliant! Clicking through the frames, they were impressed by how clear the shots were — bedrooms, dining room, the front of the house, hallway...but right in the middle of the photographs of the Jennie Wade room they made a startling discovery. There on the frame was a young woman, dark hair pulled back, high collar and lace of her dress barely touching her chin. But wrapped in her arms was a small child, long blonde curls and a white dress with satin ribbons and bows. They were completely surrounded by the white light of the angels.

The Eisenhower Room.

The Sun Room

The cheery, white wickered sun room, now a sitting room of the Farnsworth House Inn, overlooks the garden area of the grounds.

During the three day battle of early July 1863, Confederate sharpshooters were firing from the garret of the house as well as the windows of the second floor. There was an open air porch back then, which is now an enclosed sun room at the inn. The Confederate soldiers occupying the house would fire shots from their rifles, then use the brick wall for cover. When Catharine Sweney and her daughter Elizabeth came home after the battle, they ascended the steps to the second floor to find a scene of horror. Mrs. Sweney described the scene of the open air porch as a pool of congealed blood with blood splattered all over the walls. Where the brick and wood sections of the house met, she described it as looking like someone had tossed barn-red paint all around.

Visitors have reported seeing blood on the floor of the sun room. Others have experienced the smell of death, a metallic, coppery odor which accompanies a lot of blood.

In this room, a husband and wife witnessed two little boys sitting on the floor watching cartoons on the television. One child was wearing children's clothing of the late 1800s and the other little boy was dressed in clothing of the 1950s. "Could these little boys be re-enactors?" thought the couple. They inquired at the bookstore desk and realized that there were no other families staying in the house that evening. Upon listening to later voice recordings, they learned one boy's name. "Are you Jeremy?" they asked. The little boy replied with a heavy lisp, "No, my name is Billy." Perhaps Billy and Jeremy became friends in the spirit world. Both seem to be attracted to modern gadgets, including cell phones, cameras, alarm clocks and of course, the television.

The
Chamberla[in]
Room.

The
Longstreet
Room.

The
Belle Boyd
Room.

The Lincoln Room.

Helen S. Schwartz photo

The Shultz Room.

Helen S. Schwartz photo

The Sun Room.

Jim Thomas photo

Reincarnation

As told by Patti O'Day

For nearly 20 years a woman had a recurring dream involving an unknown house.

In the dream:

> I'm running down a hill — I'm on what feels like a dirt road beneath my feet — running as if my life depends on it — I need to find shelter, someplace to hide. I feel desperate, running from the enemy on the hill — loud noises, gunfire from behind — the sounds around me are deafening — I look down, I see my hands — the hands of a man — sleeves of a coat, a shade of brown. I have two companions, one on either side. A feeling of great affection and respect was over me — we are like the three musketeers — may God protect us, may we live to fight another day. We quickly enter a house — we ascend two flights of stairs — it seems our steps are in slow motion — my peripheral vision is blurred, then a sudden focus onto a door at the top of the staircase. Hot, so hot, my weapon is in order. I lay on the wooden plank floor, slide my body into position in front of a small window and prepare to fire.

The woman never knew the identity or location of the house or the circumstances of her dream. She knew nothing of the Battle of Gettysburg until visiting the town with some friends.

On that trip they were staying at the Holiday Inn and made reservations at the Farnsworth House for dinner. From their hotel, they stepped onto Baltimore Street and turned to descend the hill. The woman started to have flashbacks or quick glimpses of her dream, she slowed her pace and tried not to show her distress. As they approached the front of the house, the woman wanted to scream, "This is it! This is the house in my dreams!"

As she climbed the front steps, she kept thinking, "The entrance is different." But when she opened the door, she knew this was the same staircase, the same house and she had to fight the urge to rush up the flight of stairs and see for herself the door at the top which led into the attic. They were seated and very soon after, the woman approached Mrs. Shultz, the owner, to ask if it were possible to see the attic.

My mother, sensing something, asked me to lead the curious woman upstairs. I happened to have a key to the attic on me that day, which was unusual. As we climbed the stairs, I noticed she was very cautious, deliberate in her movements, her eyes searching, recording every detail of her surroundings. I knew something was going on so I remained quiet. As we were nearing the last landing, she looked past me and her eyes were fixed on the attic door. I asked her if she was alright since she was leaning heavily against one of the storage trunks. I sat next to her, told her to take a deep breath and I would help her walk the last set of stairs. I unlocked the door and pushed it open — she knew at last!

The "spirited" entrance of the Farnsworth House Inn.

The McFarlane Room

Named for the original owners of the Farnsworth House, this room is known for the variety of active spirits that haunt the room. It is believed that Jeremy's father visits this room quite often and relaxes on the chair in there. The spirit children enjoy playing on the twin beds like they are having their own private slumber party.

Stories from the McFarlane Room

- "We left 7 coins on the table by the door. We left 1 quarter, 3 pennies, 2 nickels and one dime to entice Jeremy. When we came back, one nickel was missing."

- "I woke up in the middle of the night...my pillow was on the floor at the end of the bed and my covers were neatly rolled down to my feet."

- "I heard some banging on the closet wall and this made me sit straight up in my bed wondering what was going on. Then I saw the rocking chair rocking back and forth hitting the wall...nobody was in the chair...."

- "I felt the air grow heavy around me like it was pressing in on me. It was heavy with a floral scent. This lasted about a minute. As I drifted off to sleep I could feel two small fingers being dragged across the rungs of the brass bed, like how a child would drag a stick along a picket fence. Then I felt the weight of a small body sit next to me. I felt the air grow cold...."

- "I bolted out of my bed when I saw him. He was a tall bearded man in a gray suit. The jacket was long and had a dark collar. He was a sorrowful looking soul. I could smell the odor of a cigar in the air for just a few seconds. Who was this man?"

- "Woke up to the laughter of children playing. There were no kids around."

- "I felt as though there were children jumping back and forth on the beds."

- "It was around midnight when I heard the laughter of a little girl in the room."

- "I heard the laughter of a little girl coming from the attic."

- "Someone whispered in my ear, *It's going to be okay...*and I knew it would be..."

- "As me and my friends headed down the stairs to check out, one by one, we heard the click of each of our doors locking behind us. It seemed as though the spirits were locking us out or locking themselves in!"

The haunted rocking chair in the McFarlane Room.

Helen S. Schwartz photo

Footsteps

As told by Patti O'Day

A gentleman and his wife arrived a bit later than anticipated and had drinks in the tavern. The wife was a bit tired and stated that she was going upstairs for a bath and bed. The husband said that he would be up in a little while, he was enjoying the live Civil War band and having a few spirits of his own. The wife, a bit annoyed, went up to the Sweney Room for a long hot bath. She later got into her nightgown, climbed into the comfortable bed, pulled the covers up to her neck and reached to turn the light out.

After what seemed like moments, she heard the door open, heard footsteps to the bed, felt someone sit on the bed next to her, heard the sound of someone undressing, even shoes hitting the floor. So that her husband wouldn't have to undress in the dark, she reached up and turned the light on, but there was no one there. She must have been dreaming. Again she turned the light off and snuggled under the covers trying to reclaim sleep.

She heard it again, the door opening, footsteps to the bed, someone sitting on the bed next to her, the sound of someone undressing...she quickly reached up and snapped on the light, and again no one. Now she is getting frightened, she knew of the house's reputation, had seen all the signs for the ghost walks, she thought of asking her husband to come up to the room but no, no, he would see that she was frightened and she would never hear the end of it. She calmed herself by thinking that there really is no such things as ghosts. It's just an old house, it must have been in one of the neighboring rooms, that's all. So she reached up, turned off the lights again and tried to go to sleep.

Again she heard the door open, footsteps to the bed, someone sitting next to her, the sounds of undressing, shoes hitting the floor. She held her breath, eyes wide, she reached up and snapped on the light. THERE AT THE FOOT OF THE BED WAS HER HUSBAND! Whew! Before she could stop herself, she blurted out what had happened. Her husband gave her one of those looks, now honey you don't have to worry about the boogey man now, I'm here, I'll protect you. She rolled on her side furious with herself for saying anything. With that she reached up and turned the light off.

It happened again! They heard the door open up, the sound of footsteps to the bed, someone sitting next to them, and the sound of someone undressing. She reached for the light, but her husband stopped her...no, let's see what happens. After a moment, they felt the covers pull back and someone laying down on the bed next to them. They quickly rolled off the other side of the bed, grabbed their luggage and left. She was chewing him out all the way to the car. You'll believe me now when I tell you something, yeah, go and protect me from the boogey man now!

Helen S. Schwartz photo

The Sweney Room, where one couple had an unexpected guest join them in bed.

The Eisenhower Room

This room was named in honor of Mamie Eisenhower, former First Lady. She was a frequent visitor to the Farnsworth House. This room has had many shenanigans going on in it. Missing room keys, sneakers being tied together, cameras and cell phones disappearing and a number of other little tricks performed by the "kids." Here's a little tip for our guests, just ask them to please return your items, they usually oblige!

STORIES FROM THE EISENHOWER ROOM

- "We heard a single knock on the door, then it opened about a foot. I checked and nobody was around."
- "Around 2 a.m., out of the corner of my eye, I saw what looked like a couple of sets of shadows "walk" by under the door in the hallway."
- "We felt someone drumming their fingers on my pillow."
- "I could smell an odor of burning wood and sweat in the room, like a soldier that has been near a campfire."
- "I woke up and saw a blue mist in the back right corner of the room, and it just flew up into the ceiling. We left a deck of cards spread out on the bed. When we came back to the room, five of the cards had been flipped over,"
- "I had put my camera on the bed for a moment. When I came back, it was nowhere to be found. I asked the spirit to return it. Then it reappeared on my bed."
- "When I went to check out, my room key was missing. I looked through everything…no key. When I checked out, I let them know it was missing." (The key was found the next day behind a curtain on the windowsill.)
- "In the middle of the night I woke up to hear a child singing a song."
- "Someone kept on untying my daughter's sneakers. Someone in the Sweney room was having the same problem."
- "I felt a finger run down the right side of my back. Later that night I felt someone tugging at my sheets."

Members of the Sweney family in front of their house circa 1897. The modern photo (below) shows how little the house has changed over the last century.

In Loving Hands

As told by Patti O'Day

It was January of 1986. My friend Debbie was visiting from Alexandria, Virginia. It was mid-day and very cold outside. The trees were heavy with ice and the water that tried to make its escape slowly formed long, glistening icicles. Since I was waiting on tables that evening I had arranged a meeting with Debbie and the "new" family who had checked into the Jennie Wade Room (now called the Eisenhower Room and at the time the private bath was located down the hall).

It was very quiet and just a few tables littered the dining room. I put everyone in the same room in front of the fireplace and wheeled our 1930s Victrola into the main room. As the melody of the *Tennessee Waltz* filtered up the staircase, I continued greeting guests and stood raving about the game pie and pumpkin fritters. Everyone had a comforting glass of hot buttered rum. We were all content even though we could still hear the tree branches gently touching the walls with icy fingers.

Unknown to our guests, Debbie and the husband of the couple began a conversation about his tour in Vietnam and his experiences as a medic. Presently he worked in a local hospital as a respiratory therapist. He had been amazed about the accounts of his mortally wounded charges in Vietnam. All could see buddies they had fought beside waiting for them to cross over. The man also had an obsession about the Civil War wounded and dying. The thought of them dying alone was most unbearable, at least he had been there for his men. Debbie was somewhat quiet about her experiences due to the simple fact that she worked for the CIA at the time.

The man's wife suddenly appeared at the door of the sitting room. Their baby who was only three months old was still in the room. She had placed him on the floor next to the bed with Victorian lace pillows at his side. She wanted her husband to keep "an ear out" for the little guy while she went to the bathroom to wash and comb her hair. All conversation started over again with no incident. A half hour passed. The mother walked back to the room and put her key in the lock and slowly opened the door.

What transpired next shocked the young woman. She screamed as if someone was standing over her child.

Quickly, Debbie and the husband flew into the room amazed at the urgency of the call. At the same time over the soft tones of the *Tennessee Waltz*, the mother's shrill cry broke through and I started running for the front staircase. I couldn't get to the room fast enough. There I saw Debbie, the man and wife and her mother standing with their mouths hanging open as the baby was being levitated at least a foot above the bed, no longer protected by the elegant Victorian pillows. Somehow I knew that he was being held by loving hands — Mary's hands — gently, so gently the child was lowered onto the bed, safe and happy. I had to hide my smile thinking they would believe that I was crazy if they read the expression on my face. Serene and proud I was of our eternal guardian of the Farnsworth House.

The scent of roses filled the air and encompassed us. I found myself speechless. All I could mumble were the words, "It's okay. Whoever has him feels that he is safer on the bed than on the floor." The mother did not seem so sure, but as the baby was being fussed over, I looked into those knowing little eyes and he smiled at me.

The Custer Room

Named after General George Armstrong Custer who graduated last in his class at West Point in 1861. Although better known for his Indian fighting, he was a notable cavalry leader during the Battle of Gettysburg.

<small>STORIES FROM THE CUSTER ROOM</small>

- "Around 2 a.m. I awoke, something had been sitting on the edge of my bed! Then it pulled the curtain back…there was a sudden whoosh that shut the curtains fast, followed by a black solid mist. Then it dissipated."

- "Between 1 and 1:30 a.m., I heard a clicking noise as if someone was playing with the lock. Every time I looked up it would stop. I would lay back down and it would start again. The spirit was playing a game and having fun with me."

- "While in the Mourning Theater, I placed a quarter on the casket. When I returned to my room, a quarter was found on my bed!"

- "I stepped into the shower. Two minutes later the chain on the toilet started swinging back and forth, knocking into the wall every time. Then the lights flickered and I totally freaked out!"

- "I was woken by the whisper of a female voice — I could not understand what she said."

- "Footsteps, all night long I heard footsteps in the room and I saw fleeting shadows near the curtains."

- "The eyes of the deer head on the wall kept following me. Finally I had to throw a towel over his head so he would stop staring at me."

- "My toothpaste disappeared from the bathroom. I chose to believe it was a ghost. Hope they enjoy their new minty fresh smile!"

The Lincoln Room

Named for the 16th President of the United States, this room is known for it's variety of spirituous happenings. The mid-nineteenth century in the United States was an age of spiritualism. First Lady, Mary Todd Lincoln continually sought the spirit of her precious son Willie through séances and spiritual consultations.

STORIES FROM THE LINCOLN ROOM

- "I heard what sounded like a ball drop, then roll as if it was on a hard wood floor. It went on all night long."

- "I repeatedly smelled the scent of roses. My girlfriend claimed that someone rubbed her feet."

- "I heard a thumping sound. It sounded like someone taking a box down the stairs — however, there are no stairs near our room, just a fake circular stairway that leads to nowhere."

- "I was in the shower facing the far wall when I saw a shadow. The shadow moved and it was gone."

- "We heard breathing and a young child's voice. Hopefully it was Jeremy."

- "We heard the heavy sound of a cat purring in our room."

The Jennie Wade Room

This room was named in honor of Gettysburg resident, Mary Virginia "Jennie" Wade, the only civilian killed during the battle of Gettysburg. It is believed that the 20 year old woman was struck down in her sister's kitchen by the bullet of a Confederate sharpshooter at post in the garret of the Farnsworth House. On occasion we have had guests actually see the spirit of Jennie Wade and actually speak to her in many of the rooms.

STORIES FROM THE JENNIE WADE ROOM

- "We could smell a very strong odor of Earl Grey Tea. It was very late, we heard rustling, a bell ring twice and the sound of shuffling feet. My mom's toothbrush went missing as well. Jeremy?"

- "I was unnerved by the painting of the staring monkey. I woke up in the middle of the night and the monkey vanished from the painting."

- "2:45 a.m. We heard a loud crash in the bathroom. I found my cup on the floor, which had slammed into the doorway. My toothbrush was in the cup when I went to bed. I found it lying on the side of the sink."

- "I came in late and was too tired to shower. The following morning I found that someone had used my towels. They were crumpled and damp. The lights in the bathroom kept on flickering also."

- "2:06 a.m. I am woken by a long squeal like a hungry kitten mewing. I felt something scurry and rub against my leg. Something with a stride, too big for a mouse, a cat perhaps...but the only cat in the room is stuffed. In the bathroom, my towel kept falling on the floor."

Morning, Feb. 16th, 2005
Farnsworth House Inn
Jennie Wade Room

Three of us stayed at the Farnsworth House in the Jenny Wade Room...here to celebrate a birthday and the present was a night at the Farnsworth House. This morning I awoke early to take photos around town while my friend and her daughter slept in a bit before breakfast. While photographing the Friend to Friend monument and then walking over to the Visitor Center I received a call from my friend asking me in a kind of a scared tone.... "Is this a joke?" I answered... "What?" She said, "The coins I threw on the night table are stacked up....did you do this? We didn't...did you do this to scare us?" I was stunned and said, "no...I didn't. Keep them there as is, I want a photo of this." I told the people in the bookstore at the Visitor Center about the call I had just gotten and they said, "Jeremy."

I went back to the room and photographed the stacks...my friends' daughter said that during the night she felt someone touch her hand. Here is the photo...and I must say...none of us put our change on the table neatly stacked like this."

As told by Helen S. Schwartz

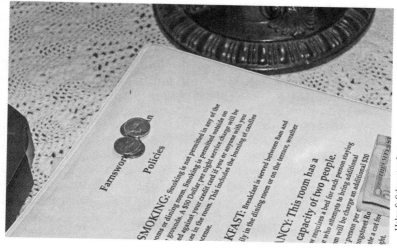

Helen S. Schwartz photo

The Belle Boyd Room

Named after the notorious Confederate spy, the Belle Boyd Room is known for it's very "TIDY" spirits. They pack your bags, fold your clothing and like to linger in the beautiful bathroom and shower area where they fold your towels and stack them for you.

STORIES FROM THE BELLE BOYD ROOM

- "I went to take a shower. I placed my comb and nightgown on the bench near the shower. I got out of the shower and discovered that my comb and nightgown disappeared! After twenty minutes of searching, I found my folded nightgown and comb in my empty tote bag."

- "After eating, we returned to our room, laid the key on the bed and started getting ready to go out. When we were ready to leave, we could not find the key! We had to go to the bookstore to get another key. We returned later and still could not find the key. We returned after an evening out and found that our key reappeared. It was next to the stuffed cat on the little bed along with two pieces of candy!"

- "We were carrying our bags to the room and sat them on the bed. We went back to the car to get more things. When we returned to our room, we found our bags were neatly tucked under the bed!"

- "We went out to dinner and when we returned, we found my husband's shirts hanging up. They were draped over the chair when we left the room."

The Longstreet Room

This room was named after Confederate General James Longstreet who was also known as Lee's "War Horse." The spirits in this room love electronics and must enjoy watching television. Keep you cell phones and cameras close to you and leave some popcorn for Billy, Jeremy and Little Cissy, they love to watch cartoons!

STORIES FROM THE LONGSTREET ROOM

- "We were awakened by the bathroom trash can sliding across the floor and hitting the wall."

- "We left a light on in the room and upon returning, the light had been turned off. Later that evening we returned again and the T.V. was on! There was a heavy feeling in the air…"

- "We came back in to find the bathroom light on — we had turned it off. The T.V. turned itself on."

- "I had the sensation of something touching my cheek as I slept. I woke up and nobody was there."

- "I was sleeping on a cot at the end of the bed. At one point it felt like something was walking across me and sat down near my legs to watch T.V. It felt like a cat was on the bed. I was too scared to look but got a chill down my body."

- "When we came back to the room, the T.V. was on. I also saw a shadow cover the bottom left corner of the window. I felt like someone was sitting at the edge of the bed and shaking it."

- "We turned the lights off before we left. After dinner, we returned and the lights were on."

The Shultz Room

Named after the present day owners of the establishment, this room is filled with fun loving spirits that enjoy "visiting" with their new guests.

STORIES FROM THE SHULTZ ROOM

- "The door knob in the room jiggled 3 times. The lampshade above the bed was swinging back and forth furiously!"

- "We heard drums tapping outside our room…"

- "I was just getting in bed and reaching up to turn the light off, when the bed suddenly lurched like someone had kicked the frame. Later that night, I saw in my peripheral vision a floating head next to the bed."

- "Very strange and bazaar happenings in this room. I saw a man with a beard staring at me, then he vanished!"

- "I felt the rustle of stiff fabric alongside the bed, like someone wearing a long full dress."

- "We heard footsteps in the interior hallway and next to the bed going into the bathroom area. I heard thumping footsteps going down the stairs."

- "Something kept touching me playfully. It would pick at my clothes, move my pillows and my fingers. It was like a child who wanted to play with me."

- "I saw a line of light shaped like the head and shoulders of a person near the window."

- "Someone tugged on the back of my shirt and I heard the faint sound of a music box playing."

- "I saw a man with a beard and long gray suit staring at my wife as she slept."

The Chamberlain Room

This room is named after Colonel Joshua Lawrence Chamberlain, a true believer in the spirits. It is said that Chamberlain's men, and some of the captured Alabama boys, believed that the ghost of General Washington fought with Chamberlain that day in July, 1863.

In great deeds something abides. On great fields something stays. Forms change and pass; bodies disappear, but spirits linger, to consecrate ground for the vision-place of souls. And reverent men and women from afar, and generations that know us not and that we know not of, heart-drawn to see where and by whom great things were suffered and done for them, shall come to this deathless field to ponder and dream; And lo! the shadow of a mighty presence shall wrap them in its bosom, and the power of the vision pass into their souls.

Joshua Lawrence Chamberlain,
October 3, 1889,
Gettysburg, Pa.

Stories from the Chamberlain Room

- "At 3:30 p.m. I was awaken to the sound of wood chopping or some kind of banging outside behind the room. It grew louder and louder to the point that it drove me crazy."

- "I placed my new Confederate soldier teddy bear on the bedside table while I was gone for the evening. When we returned, the bear was underneath the bed...very strange...."

- "I heard a deep, raspy, airy voice whisper in my ear, *HELP ME!* I froze, I felt the hair on my neck and back stand up and I became extremely cold. Again, the voice continued to say, *Please before you leave today*...and his voice faded."

- "We heard the mewing of a cat in our room. We saw nothing, but when we came back, there was a circular indentation on the bed like a sleeping cat would leave. The spot was warm also."

The Calico Cat

As told by Patti O'Day

A young man and woman checked into the Chamberlain Room. The man was specific at check-in that there were no "common rooms" with cats roaming at will, he was highly allergic to them! The bookstore assured him that the only cats in residence were fake cats covered with rabbit fur. He seemed content and followed the young girl to the Baltimore Street location of his room.

After close inspection which included checking the closet and under the bed, he was sure that there were no four leggers lurking around in his room. His wife decided to take a shower and she left the closet door open to gain easy access to her clothing. The man found a nice comfy spot on the bed and closed his eyes.

Shortly after, he heard the creaking of a door opening very slowly as if calculated by the individual seeking passage through the opening as if it did not want to disturb the occupants of the bed or bath.

The man giggled to himself remembering some of the inn's stories but he was staying in the new section, a new building, he need not worry. Little did he know that a small calico cat was making her way into his domain, his bedroom. He saw a blur of mottled dark fur and two small paws with white tips. He bolted in his bed, glanced at the feline again and yelled for his wife. She appeared half dressed, hair tousled, at the doorway. "What in God's name are you yelling about?" she said.

"There's a cat in this room and it just went under the bed!" he replied. The woman turned around and returned to the bathroom. The man began to smile and think to himself, "Oh boy! I'm losing it!" He then felt a presence and turned, there sitting on the carpet next to the bed was female calico cat with one paw in the air and the unmistakable sound of purring filled the room.

All Hallow's Eve on the Radio

As told by Patti O'Day

In October of 1999, the crew of WQSR-FM decided to broadcast live at the haunted Farnsworth House Inn just for the fun of it. Steve Rouse and crew came in from the Baltimore based radio station with no expectations of seeing a ghost. It would be a Halloween they would never forget.

Steve Rouse, the leader of the morning radio show and the WQSR staff had full run of the inn and stayed in the haunted rooms. The crew stayed up most of the night listening for creaking doors, mysterious footsteps and ghostly activities. Maynard G. and Steve spent a substantial amount of time in the garret of the house where Confederate sharpshooters held their post during the Battle of Gettysburg. Right away they discovered that the door kept on opening up even though they secured the door numerous times. Needless to say, this started to creep them out.

Helen S. Schwartz photo

The antique baby carriage that moves on its own.

While there, the men noticed an antique metal baby carriage that sat on the landing of the second floor near the stairs heading up to the garret. When they came downstairs, Maynard noticed that the carriage had been moved. It was facing in a different direction with the two front wheels resting on the steps leading up to the garret. It seemed as though someone tried to push the carriage up the stairs and ran out of energy.

The following morning, Steve and Maynard did their broadcast from the cellar. While in the cellar, they experienced the stench of death, the smell of rotting flesh. The group agreed that the odor came from the "catacombs," a small tunnel like area with a dirt floor. It was only accessible through a side door of the theater.

Maynard, a lady clairvoyant and two ghost hunters entered the narrow tunnel. The clairvoyant had a bad feeling and urged them to get out immediately. Everyone headed toward the exit and Maynard felt something tugging at his pant leg. After he exited the catacombs, he found a muddy handprint on his pant leg and he heard the sound of a crying child coming from the tunnel. The crew of WQSR in Baltimore couldn't wait to pack there bags and get out of the house!

During the 1920s, William H. Tipton produced this postcard entitled
"Mrs. Black's Lodging House, 401 Baltimore St., Gettysburg, Pa."
On the reverse, the caption read: "BLACK'S LODGING HOUSE
furnishes splendid ACCOMMODATIONS for TOURISTS. This
house was occupied by Confederate sharpshooters during the battle
of Gettysburg on July 1, 2, and 3, 1863, which made it a target for
the Union troops on East Cemetery Hill. Scores of bullet holes mark
the end shown here as well as other parts of the house."

Original "Sleepy Hollow Lodging" sign hangs in the stairway of the Farnsworth House Inn. Photo courtesy Helen S. Schwartz.

Other books available from Farnsworth House Military Impressions:

*In the Eye of the Storm:
The Farnsworth House & the
Battle of Gettysburg.*

*Is She Kate?
The Woman Major General
John Fulton Reynolds Left
Behind.*

The Civil War
Commander series.
Each volume presents the
biography of a significant
Civil War personality.

Coming Soon:

*Gettysburg's Haunted Address
Volume II*

The Historic FARNSWORTH HOUSE offers a Victorian Bed & Breakfast, formal and informal dining, a tavern, relic shop, book store, and their popular Mourning Theatre. For more information visit our website at:

www.farnsworthhouseinn.com

Or write to:

FARNSWORTH HOUSE
401 Baltimore Street
Gettysburg, PA 17325